Making The Connection
The Power of Praise & Worship

Carla Burton

Contents

Dedication

This book is dedicated to my husband, J. Kurtis Burton and to my daughter, Caitlin Elizabeth.

Kurtis, for over 25 years we have *done* ministry together and it has been the greatest adventure of my life. I am blessed to be married and work alongside you in the calling of God!

Caitlin, your Dad and I truly understood the favor and blessing of God when you were born on April 24, 1994. We have watched you grow into a beautiful, amazing young lady with wonderful dreams for your future. We are honored to see your love for God and others and know that you are the greatest *project* we have ever accomplished together!

Preface

Worship is the very reason that we were created! The entire design and plan of God was to create us so that we could find connection (worship) with Him! When I was a child growing up as a missionary kid in the Philippines, I was amazed to see the beautiful worship that came from people who had nothing. Their connection with God was never based on their comfort or their wealth, because so often they had neither in their lives. It was simply from an understanding of who God was and how important He was to them. When I returned to America, I realized that many of our people were not truly making a connection with God in worship and praise. It became a heartbeat of my life to try and help us understand how beautiful and powerful it was for a Christian to make that connection. And with that thought in mind, this book began in my spirit.

The purpose of this book is so that anyone, no matter their level and walk with God, can pick this up and have a new understanding of why and how to connect to God in worship and praise. There are many books out there with deeper theological studies regarding the topic of praise and worship in the Bible and I encourage you to read them as well. However, if you would like the perspective of a missionary kid who learned to connect to God in grass-roofed churches; or the perspective of a young lady who God used in praise and worship from an early age; or the perspective of a young minister's wife who started and developed the music and worship ministry at her local church; or the perspective of a pastor's wife who can see the needs of people sitting on the pew and then see the deliverance they can find in worship, then this is the book for you! I pray, as you read, the illumination that God has given me from the Word and that has been activated in my personal life, will help you to have a greater understanding of connection to God. And that you will understand how He uses the avenue of praise and worship to make that connection!

Introduction

In the *Beginning*

Darkness is everywhere. Only two things exist in the darkness: the holy presence of Almighty God and the innumerable angels He has created. Suddenly, His voice rings out, "Let there be light." Immediately there is a bright glowing object hanging in the dark void. Suddenly, it begins! From one corner of the universe a sound, like the roar of voices in a football stadium during a Sunday afternoon game! What is this sound? What is the cacophony of noise? It is the voice of the angels, shouting out the praise of the God who has just created something from nothing! This was the moment that they had been created for. This was their ultimate purpose – to simply reflect the glory and majesty of their God through praise! And oh, this praise service was *just beginning!*

Each time God created something else, the chorus of voices cried out in adulation at His handiwork. Can you imagine this praise service? For six days, there are only three things happening: God's voice speaking creation into existence, the creation being birthed, and then the ringing voices of millions of angels exalting the Creator.

In Job 38:4-7, God gives us insight into that wonderful first week of creation. He asks Job to account for his whereabouts when God measured and molded the earth. He tells Job that He doesn't remember him being present when *"the morning stars sang together, and all the sons of God shouted for joy...."* The first praise and worship service! Wouldn't it have been awesome to stand in the darkness in the midst of the angels and hear those voices reverberate around you in praise?

But we were also created to give God praise and worship. Because of this, we, as God's creation, needs to recreate that atmosphere of praise and worship every day. Our hearts need to find a way to connect with the Almighty presence of God each day. In this book, I want to try to help you understand the importance of praise and worship. We are on the stage of life, involved in the greatest dress rehearsal of all time. Now is our chance to learn how to praise and worship so that we will be ready to stand with the 24 elders, the beasts, and the angels around the throne of God. Revelation 5:12 says that they cried out with a loud voice, *"Worthy is the Lamb that was slain to receive power, and riches, and wisdom, and strength, and honor, and glory, and blessing."*

Open the pages of this book and gain knowledge, and then open your heart and obey. This book can revolutionize your life, your church, and your eternity.

Chapter 1

Creation *Calling*

We, the human race, must understand that we were designed and created to worship God. This was the very first purpose for our creation and existence. Revelations 4:9-11 gives us an insight into the atmosphere surrounding the throne of God. *"And when those beasts give glory and honour and thanks to him that sat on the throne, who liveth for ever and ever, The four and twenty elders fall down before him that sat on the throne, and worship him that liveth for ever and ever, and cast their crowns before the throne, saying, Thou art worthy, O Lord, to receive glory and honour and power: **for thou hast created all things, and for thy pleasure they are and were created.**"* For His pleasure, for His worship, for His glory, we were created! Every person alive has the same **creation calling.** This is the entire, complete reason that they were created and that is to worship and give glory to God. Isaiah helped us understand this in Isaiah 43:7, *"Even every one that is called by my name: for I have **created him for my glory**, I have formed him; yea, I have*

9

made him." Our true calling is to worship! This is our *creation calling*!

Within each of us are different gifts and talents. Some people are driven and passionate, some people are gentle and creative, some people are kind and meek, others are full of life and laughter. And each of these traits should lead us to serve and work for the Kingdom of God in a special way. This is our *gifted calling*. This is something designed in our DNA that helps us further the Kingdom of God and usually translates into our chosen secular careers as well. This gifting is given at creation for our use to further His Kingdom first. But our gifted calling is not the same in everyone. It is as different in each person as our thumbprints or eye color. And our gifted calling and our creation calling are two different things. Even though our gifted calling is different, every person has the **same** *creation calling* – and that is to worship! Psalm 29:1-2 says it like this, *"Give unto the LORD, O ye mighty, give unto the LORD glory and strength. **Give unto the LORD the glory due unto his name**; worship the LORD in the beauty of holiness."* We are commanded to give unto God the glory that is due Him. He is due this simply because **He is God**!! There doesn't need to be any other reason to praise and worship Him. Simply because He is and He exists, we should operate in our creation calling and give Him praise. Psalm 95:1-7 helps us understand this concept, *"O come, let us sing unto the LORD: let us make a joyful noise to the rock of our salvation. Let us come before his presence with thanksgiving, and make a joyful noise unto him with psalms. For the LORD is a great God, and a great King above all gods. In his hand are the deep places of the earth: the strength of the hills is his also. The sea is his,* *and he made it: and his hands formed the dry land. **O come, let us worship and bow down: let us kneel before the LORD our maker.** For he is our God; and we are the people of his pasture, and the sheep of his hand."* We need to learn to worship simply because He is our maker and Creator *because* this is what we were created to do.

In fact there is only one *requirement* in the Bible to praise and worship God – **breath**! Psalm 150:6, *"Let every thing that hath **breath** praise the LORD. Praise ye the LORD."* David tells us that if you have breath in your body then that is all you need to be able to exercise your *creation calling*, because where did this breath come from originally anyway?

In Genesis 2:7 the Bible tells us the story of the creation of man. It says, *"And the LORD God formed man of the dust of the ground, and breathed into his nostrils the breath of life; and man became a living soul."* The very breath that you have came from God Himself. And worship is simply that breath, the life that God gave of Himself to us, desiring to return back to its Creator. And therefore, when we open our mouths and willingly send that breathe back to it's Creator through worship, we feel complete and whole because we are fulfilling our created purpose. David understands that it is only while we are *living* that we can give worship and praise to God. Psalm 146:1-2, *" Praise ye the LORD. Praise the LORD, O my soul. While I live will I praise the LORD: I will sing praises unto my God while I have any being."* He says while I *live* and while I have *any being*. Oh, that we could grasp this concept and apply it to our lives everyday. This is why each morning you should get up with a praise on your lips. From the moment that you are aware of the first breath you take that morning, you should send that breath back to its Creator in worship and praise.

This is why only *living beings* can produce praise and worship. Inanimate objects *cannot* worship without a living being. They are simply tools. They alone, by themselves, cannot worship God. Worship songs unsung are simply poems. An instrument unplayed produces nothing. A praise word unspoken is simply a hope unfulfilled. These tools need a living, breathing person to use them to worship.

David in Psalm 150:2-5 says over and over again that we praise God *with and upon* instruments but that they, by themselves, do **not** praise God alone. *"Praise him for his mighty acts: praise him according to his excellent greatness. Praise him **with** the sound of the trumpet: praise him **with** the psaltery and harp. Praise him **with** the timbrel and dance: praise him **with** stringed instruments and organs. Praise him **upon** the loud cymbals: praise him **upon** the high sounding cymbals."* What is actually giving praise here is the *person* who is playing the instrument, not the instrument.

When the children of Israel victoriously came through the Red Sea and saw their enemy, the Egyptians, drowned, they decided that this deserved praise to God for their deliverance. In Exodus 15:20 the Bible tells us, *"And Miriam the prophetess, the sister of Aaron, took a timbrel in her hand; and all the women went out after her with timbrels and with dances."* But the tambourine could not give God any praise for the victory without Miriam. In fact praise did not start taking place in this story until Exodus 15:21 where it says, *"And Miriam answered them, Sing ye to the LORD, for he hath triumphed gloriously; the horse and his rider hath he thrown into the sea."* When Miriam began to speak, then praise began to take place. The tambourine was an inanimate object that needed a living, being person to pick it up and use it as a tool to introduce worship.

When it came time for Joshua and the children of Israel to see a victory at Jericho, God gave them a unique plan. He asked them to march for 6 days around the city one time. Joshua instructed the people that during these times of marching, *the people* were to be silent, but the trumpets would still sound (Joshua 6:6-9). However, the people were instructed by Joshua to keep silent. Joshua 6:10, *"And Joshua had commanded the people, saying, Ye shall not shout, nor make any noise with your voice, neither shall any word proceed out of your mouth, until the day I bid you shout; then shall ye shout."*

We read in Joshua 6:12-14, *"And Joshua rose early in the morning, and the priests took up the ark of the LORD. And seven priests bearing seven trumpets of rams' horns before the ark of the LORD went on continually, and blew with the trumpets: and the armed men went before them; but the rereward came after the ark of the LORD, the priests going on, and blowing with the trumpets. And the second day they compassed the city once, and returned into the camp: so they did six days"* How interesting that on days 1-6, the instruments played but the people were silent, **and there was no victory**. But it wasn't until Joshua 6:16 that we see something different happen. *"And it came to pass at the seventh time, when the priests blew with the trumpets, Joshua said unto the people, Shout; for the LORD hath given you the city."* This time the living, breathing people begin to use their *created calling* to praise God for the victory! When they did what they were called to do then something happened

13

– VICTORY!! If the victory was in the instruments, then it would have happened on day one at the first blast of the trumpet. Instruments are simply tools to announce the entrance of praise and worship. They are the call that it is time to get up and activate yourself into the presence of God. We see this played out in Joshua 6:20, *"So the people shouted when the priests blew with the trumpets: and it came to pass, when the people heard the sound of the trumpet, and the people shouted with a great shout, that the wall fell down flat, so that the people went up into the city, every man straight before him, and they took the city."* It was when the people shouted that the victory came. Because it was the *created calling* being activated, which God will always hear and respond to.

So it should never be hard to give praise and worship back to God, because this was the reason we were created. There is something within each of us that cries out to give this to God. This is why when we come to church and we don't respond in worship, we leave feeling empty and wanting. But when we do allow our creation calling to take place and respond, then we leave feeling fulfilled and complete.

I encourage you today to start walking *daily* in your creation calling. Find a place, find a time and open your mouth and send the borrowed breath of God back to its rightful owner in praise and worship!

Chapter 2

Created *to Choose*

For many years, I have heard that the angels were created to worship God. I agree with this statement; however, in studying the Word of God, I discovered that they were also created with a *choice* to worship.

In Hebrews 1:6, the Apostle says, *"And let all the angels of God worship Him."* God wanted someone to exalt Him, so He created beings called angels. They fulfill many roles for Him. They are worshippers, messengers, ministering spirits, and warriors, but His ultimate plan for them is to continually worship Him. There are many references in the Bible to them doing just that. For instance, the angels worshipped at creation (Job 38), and they worshipped at the birth of Jesus (Hebrews 1:6 and Luke 2:13-14).

Ezekiel 28:11-20 tells about the creation of a particular angel named Lucifer. He was created so grandly that the Bible says he was "perfect" in his ways. Verse 13 states that every beautiful and precious gem covered him. His beauty shone like the sun as he walked up and down around the throne of God. The last part of verse 13 reveals that he was also created with tabrets (timbrels or tambourines) and pipes. Tabrets were used in the temple to promote praise and worship. The "pipes" that are spoken of in verse 13 have to do with his vocal cords. He was given a beautiful voice to worship and praise God. But the very things that were given to him to produce praise and worship became the very things that caused his downfall. In verse 16 the Bible accuses Lucifer of his sin. It states, *"By the multitude of thy merchandise they have filled the midst of thee with violence, and thou hast sinned."* He was filled with violence and jealousy. As the chief archangel of praise, Lucifer was created with an ability to speak or sing praise to God. But he was also created with something else--*the ability to choose whom he would worship.*

Perhaps the saddest scripture in all the Word of God is found in Ezekiel 28:15. It reveals that Lucifer was perfect in all his ways *until* iniquity was found in Him. He made a choice to give his praise to someone else besides his Creator. His heart became lifted up, and he turned the praise from Almighty God to himself.

We are created in the image of God. When God molded the dust and breathed the breath of life into the first man in Genesis 2:7, He had already had a conference with the angels in Genesis 1:26. He told them He was going to make man in "our" image and after "our" likeness. Throughout the scriptures we see that there is a thin line separating humans from the angels. Paul tells us in Hebrews 2:7 that Christ in his humanity was made a "little lower than the angels," indicating that men and angels are similar in many ways, yet different in a few.

We could spend much time on the differences between the angels and humanity; however, I want to dwell on the similarities. ***Both were created by God with an instinct to praise and worship someone or something. And both were created with the will to decide whom or*** *what to worship.* There are only two choices when it comes to praise and worship: Either you worship God or you make something else your "god" and worship it. It could be yourself or some *thing*. Worship of anyone or anything besides the living God is what Solomon called "vanity," a thing that seems important but really is nothing. That was the choice that Lucifer had in heaven, and he chose himself above God.

The greatest liberty in the world is freedom of choice. America was founded upon this principle and has spent every decade since defending this liberty. Every major war America has fought has been to continue freedom in our country or to try to bring it to other nations. The heart and mind of every man strives for freedom. No one likes to be enslaved or told they cannot do something. We were created with a free will by God that we express through choices we make.

In the dominion of praise and worship, we must understand that we were created with a desire to give praise to something. We look for things in our life to exalt and magnify.

People in the world have shown us that they are praising themselves above God. The world has adopted the philosophy of secular humanism. They believe themselves to be "gods" and as such deserve all the praise. They try to produce it through many avenues, such as sports, fame, beauty, talent, and education. The world has brought the concept of praise to a new level. Actors and actresses determine the way people in the world act, talk, and dress. Athletes are placed on pedestals and worshipped as gods while people adopt their mode of dress, conduct, and attitude. From every movie, every television screen, and every major sports event, we watch the world determine the direction of our society. Young girls give their bodies to bulimia and anorexia to worship the figures of models and actresses. Young boys smoke, drink, and adopt the language of actors and sports figures. The world is telling us that we can praise ourselves no matter the consequences.

Even Christians can be guilty of praising our own selfish desires before God. In Exodus 20, God reveals His greatest condition for relationship with Him--placing no other god before Him. Yet we place jobs, family relationships, time, and children before Him. We attend church, but we don't spend the time there giving Him the praise He is due. We obey the Word to an extent, but don't allow the Word to transform us. We can simply go through the motions of placing Him first, or we can make a choice to praise Him in all things.

No matter the situation or circumstance, we must dwell in a spirit of praise. I have learned this through many difficult times. In a five-year time period, my husband and I lost six immediate family members. In 1996, we lost my mother-in-law and my grandfather. In 1997, we lost my grandmother and my mother. In 1998, we lost my father-in-law, and in 2001, we lost our nine-day-old baby girl. I have come to realize that the circumstance cannot affect my praise. I must make a choice to praise Him through all things! Remember, it is not how many answers you know *after* the test; what you know only counts while you are taking the test. I tell many people that praise counts while you are going through the trial or test. It doesn't matter if you can praise Him when the storm is over; anyone can do that. The only thing that matters is that you praise Him during the storm!

You were created to choose *whom* you will praise. Today you are praising God or something else you have placed before Him. Check your life. Someone once said if you let me look at how a man spends his time and money, I will tell you what is most important to him. What would your life say about you? Will it show you making a choice to praise God in all things, or will it say you worship yourself above all other things?

Throughout the scriptures we see many men in the valley of decision. A test, a storm, a trial has come upon them, and it is time to decide how they will react. Joseph never stopped praising God through every test. While David, the chosen King, was running from Saul, he never stopped praising the Lord. The early church, persecuted by the rulers of that day, continued to teach, praise, and deliver the Word of God. Paul and Silas in Acts 16:25 were at "midnight," the very darkest hour of their lives, yet they sang praises unto God.

Make a choice today to start praising God through everything. Let praise revolutionize your life and relationship with God. Praise produces power, so make the right choice and praise!

Chapter 3

The *Universal Language*

It is a great thought to consider that of all the languages in the world there is only one word that is common to them all--"hallelujah." Even though the spelling is different from French to German, the meaning is still the same. The word "hallelujah" means a song or shout of praise to God. So no matter the country, no matter the language, there is a word that unifies us all. Hallelujah, a praise word, is the one word that God has given to every tongue.

The story of the Tower of Babel in the book of Genesis describes how God confused the common language of the people, resulting in many different tongues. But as you read more of the story you realize this was all about praise. Genesis 11:4 tells us that the reason the people were building the tower was to "make us a name." The instant that you try to take God's praise, you will always bring confusion into the mixture. When God realized that they were going to take the praise due Him for themselves He took action, confounding their languages and scattering them throughout the entire world. To this day, we are divided by our languages.

There has never been an entire reversal of Babel; however, we do see that in Acts 2 on the Day of Pentecost, God introduced a new language that everyone could speak. When the 120 in the upper room began to speak with tongues, a new language was born. Today the church is unified through this language. We can see an example of this in Acts 10 when the household of Cornelius, a Gentile, began to speak with other tongues. Acts 10:44-46 shows us that the Jews who came with Peter were astonished to see the Gentiles receive the Holy Ghost and the only way they knew this was, *"For they heard them speak with tongues, and magnify God."* There were no two groups of people more separate than the Jews and the Gentiles. They had no fellowship with one another. Yet, here we see the language of tongues unifying them for the first time in the scripture.

Anytime a group of people no matter their differences join together to praise God, there will always be unity. Praise brings unity to the church. When we travel to countries around the world, we may never be able to communicate in their language. Yet we may enter a church service together and begin praising God, and all differences disappear. Lifting up God erases all lines of differences, because suddenly the focus is not on us but on Him. If we can continually remember that praise is about Him, then we will create a spirit of unity in the church.

When you are exalting and magnifying God, you are focusing the attention on God. His Spirit will bring unity to the church through praise and worship.

The most important thing to remember is that there is only one word in any language that is universal and that is a praise word. There is great unity in praise.

Revelation 7:9 describes a great multitude of people, but notice that the scripture says, *". . . of all nations, and kindreds, and people, and tongues."* And they stood before the Lamb, clothed in white robes with palm branches in their hands, worshipping and praising

God. They were joined by angels, the beast, and the elders, and they just magnified God together.

If you are in a situation of conflict, then I suggest that you join together with your fellow believers and begin to praise the Lord. Instead of focusing on your differences with each other, focus on the one thing you can agree on: God is worthy of your praise. If your church is having a problem with unity, spend more time in your service promoting true praise and worship. When people praise God together, it brings a strong spirit of unity.

Let the universal language of your church be praise and worship unto God.

Chapter 4

Who *Is It All About?*

True praise is uninhibited! We must remember whom we are praising. I am often frustrated, as a worship leader, as I try to help people respond in praise and worship. Many of them will come to me later and say, "I really wanted to get involved, but I was worried about what others would think or say about me." The instant I hear that I know this person doesn't understand *whom* praise is all about. Praise is about God! We don't deserve the praise, and like Lucifer, we have to be careful not to try to steal the praise of God. Remember that your goal is to magnify God and Him alone!

The word "magnify" means to make something bigger, larger, or better able to be seen. If you are reading and the words are small you will need to magnify them to be able to truly see and understand them. This does not mean you go in and change the font to something larger;

but to magnify means you pick up something and place it over the words to help others see them larger.

We must understand that God is great, wonderful, and almighty, but our job is to magnify or to make God larger and bigger and better able to be seen by those around us. God does not need us to change Him to make Him larger and better able to be seen by others. He just needs us to magnify *who He already is!* Maintain this thought as you enter your next worship service. Every praise action (singing, dancing, clapping, leaping), and every worship word should be all about Him and how you can help those around you understand Him better.

Psalm 9:1 expresses this thought completely: *"I will praise thee, O LORD, with my whole heart; **I will shew forth all thy marvelous works.**"* Our job is to show His marvelous works, not our own. As I praise God in a service, I often try to remember all the things He has done for me. I will thank Him for being my healer, deliverer, provider, shield, protection, strength, hope, salvation, peace, joy, and contentment. As you begin to praise God and remember all the wonderful things He has done for you, your focus begins to move from yourself to your God.

Many people use the excuse that they are just self-conscious. A red flag should rise up in your spiritual man the instant you use this excuse. Being "self-conscious" means it's all about you and nothing about Him. The word "self" has to do with anything surrounding you and "conscious" means to be aware. "Self-conscious" means to only be aware of you. Now let me ask you again, who is praise all about? Exodus lets us know that He is a jealous God and won't allow His praise to be given to anyone or anything else. (See Exodus 20:5 and 34:14.)

Lucifer fell like lightening from heaven because he tried to steal God's praise. How can we be blessed when our time of praise is more about us than Him? Close your eyes, focus your mind on God, remember all that He has done for you, and use scripture in your praise. Get your mind on Him, and give Him the praise due to Him!

I must confess that as a pastor's wife and worship leader I am often frustrated by some people's lack of response to God in worship. Being privy to information concerning events in their lives, I see them still sit silently in church and not respond in worship. You never read in the Bible where anyone worshipped God silently. The Spirit of God moves in different ways (excited, shouting praise or soft, gentle worship), but it will always demand a response from you.

Praise and worship is not a SPECTATOR sport! There is no true worship when I am simply an observer and not a participant. In the New Testament, Jesus *never* healed spectators. He only healed those that participated and asked for His help. The blind men followed him worshipping and asking for healing. The woman with the issue of blood pushed her way to the front and touched Him seeking healing. Perhaps, why we have churches full of people who are sick in body, mind and spirit, is because they are simply there as a spectator. They come and leave the same way they came in because they never took the time to get His attention and ask for healing and deliverance. Our churches have become hospitals with piped in music to only make the sick feel a little better before they leave. We have become stadiums full of people who sit, but never take the field and actually earn the reward that the players receive. And they come and sit on our pews each week with financial, spiritual, physical, mental and emotional needs but never pick up the tool that can lift them out of their situation.

I have found that activating the body often activates the spirit of man. The Bible gives us a praise handbook by telling us different ways to activate ourselves in praise. First of all, singing is one of the best forms of praise. Psalm 47:6-7 commands, *"Sing praises to God, sing praises: sing praises unto our King, sing praises. For God is the King of all the earth: sing ye praises with understanding."* This best tells us why we praise Him because He is the King of all the earth. My friend, Angie Clark, recently made a profound statement. She said that there are not two kingdoms on the earth. For there to be two kingdoms there would have to be two kings. We know that isn't true because God said there is no one beside Him. There is only one King, Jesus Christ, and the other is just an imitator. Satan doesn't rule a kingdom; he rules a band of rag-tag, rebellious, expelled former angels. Our King is omnipresent--He can be everywhere at the same time. Satan is limited to one place at one time. Our King is omnipotent--He has all power in heaven and on earth. Satan is limited to simply what he had in heaven--his voice. He is limited by the Word of God and the resistance of a true believer. James 4:7 states, *"Resist the devil, and he will flee from you."* Our King is omniscient--He knows all things, even our beginning from our ending. Satan didn't even have the sense to know that killing Jesus would ultimately bring his own downfall. He cannot see our future nor determine our future. There are not two kings, so there cannot be two kingdoms. There is the kingdom of light, and darkness is trying to surround it and snuff it out.

Knowing what we know about our King, we must praise Him with the praise He is due.

When we praise God, as He deserves, we bring condemnation upon the devil because that was His job in heaven. The Lord has allowed a creature, lower than an angel, to step up and take the angels' place in praise. I believe that when we praise the Lord out loud with singing, the devil won't stick around to hear it.

We can also praise God according to our handbook, the Bible, by clapping our hands and lifting our voices in the shout. Psalm 47:1 commands, *"O clap your hands, all ye people; shout unto God with the voice of triumph."* Praise is simply taking your physical body and using it to show outward praise unto the Lord. The easiest way is by clapping your hands. People clap to show approval, excitement, agreement, and support. When the home team players take the field, the crowd shows its approval and support by clapping. When you enter a church service, you are coming to the greatest event you will ever attend. Clap your hands unto God and show Him your approval and excitement to be in His presence. We know that if two or three believers are gathered in His name, He is already there. If your church runs more than two, then God shows up every time you come to church! Try starting your service off with a round of hand clapping. God is there, so let Him know that you are glad He is.

Shouting has often been confused in Pentecost with dancing. Shouting is using your voice to praise the Lord. Proclaiming the greatness of God with your voice puts hell on the run. I love all the scriptures in the Bible for shouting. In Joshua 6 the story of Jericho is told. In my imagination I can see the people of Jericho each day stand on the walls and watch this silent crowd of over two million people march around their city. Joshua 6:10 lets us know that they silently walked around the city, *"And Joshua had commanded the people, saying, Ye shall not shout, nor make any noise with your voice, neither shall any word proceed out of your mouth, until the day I bid you shout; then shall ye shout."* Can you imagine that last day as they marched around the walls of Jericho silently six times? I'm sure the inhabitants of Jericho thought this was just another day. But what a moment when the rams' horns began to blow and, "Joshua said unto the people, Shout; for the LORD hath given you the city." There is victory in the shout. Maybe you haven't conquered your city yet because you haven't shouted unto God for it. Pastors and worship leaders, the next time you are in service, have your church stand facing outward to each direction of your city (north, south, east, and west). Have them lift up their hands and shout unto God for giving them victory in their city. All of hell will tremble and shake before a church that knows how to shout for victory.

What about Gideon and his small band of men in Judges 7? It doesn't take a large church. Gideon started out with over 30,000, but the Lord said, "I don't have to have that many to win a battle." Just a few who are willing to shine their light and shout will be able to overcome any enemy. Deuteronomy 32:30 tells us that one can put 1,000 to flight, but if you have two, they can put 10,000 to flight. Shouting increases the faith of your people and scares the enemy at the same time. There are 61 references in the Bible to the word shout. Almost all of them refer to shouting to God for victory. If you are going through a time of trial, be the first to shout unto the Lord. Shouting brings the victory.

Dancing is in the Bible as a form of praise unto God. Dancing usually occurs when we wake up and realize what God has done or is doing for our lives. Many people think they cannot dance unless the Spirit takes them over completely and they go wild. They think dancing is flinging your arms about wildly, shaking every bobby pin loose from your hair, and clearing the whole row of seats around you. I have seen people get taken over by the Spirit in that way, but I feel that many people miss out on an opportunity to praise God because they are waiting for that moment to happen. The Bible says in I Corinthians 14:32, *"And the spirits of the prophets are subject to the prophets."* If you are a person who does not easily give over control of yourself to others, you can quench that Spirit from taking control of your body. I remember when I first learned to dance before the Lord. I had seen this wild experience in others and felt that was the only way to worship the Lord. So when I was praising God, I would feel the Spirit move upon me to dance, then I would wait for the Spirit to basically take over. It never happened. One night as I was praising God with my hands lifted and my eyes closed, a wise, dear, older saint of God approached me. Sister Betty Fraizer is a wonderful, blind, prophetess from Bro. T. L. Craft's church in Jackson, Mississippi. She had someone bring her over to me. She placed her hands upon my waist and said in my ear, "Carla, I know you want to dance. I'm here to tell you that all you have to do is move your feet." It was that simple, yet that profound. I began to move my feet and before I knew it, I was dancing all over the place. The next time you feel that surge of the Holy Ghost, just

31

start moving your feet, and guess what, you're dancing before the Lord.

A radical thought is that you can keep your eyes open and dance before the Lord. Miriam and all the women of Israel went out in Exodus 15:20 and began to dance because God had given them victory over Egypt. I don't think they were dancing with their eyes closed, but they were simply showing God in the dance thanks for the victory. In II Samuel 6:16, David was leaping and dancing before the Ark of the Covenant as it returned to Jerusalem. He was laughed at and ridiculed by his own wife, but I love David's response to her. In verse 22 he basically said, "You ain't seen nothin' yet! I will do even more vile things in your sight because I give my praise to God." I often tell people in our church, "Move your feet!" That is all you have to do to start dancing.

Leaping before the Lord is another great form of praise unto God. The great thing about leaping is that the Bible tells us that it is a recipe for joy. Luke 6:22-23 says, *"Blessed are ye, when men shall hate you, and when they shall separate you from their company, and shall reproach you, and cast out your name as evil, for the Son of man's sake. Rejoice ye in that day, and **leap for joy**: for, behold, your reward is great in heaven: for in the like manner did their fathers unto the prophets."* It doesn't say to leap because you have joy. In fact, Luke is talking about when you are going through a trial or a test. When you are being talked about, when you are depressed, when it feels like no one (even your own family) likes you, leap for joy! The word "for" means to get or to receive. When you begin to leap, then you will receive joy. If your church feels as though it has a spirit of depression or sadness upon it, have a leaping praise service and watch as God spreads joy around. Rev. Charles Hatcher, Jr., once said that the best way to make a soda can explode was to shake it up. He proceeded to jump up and down—his way of shaking his container of the Holy Ghost. It certainly produced the desired effect: the entire congregation broke out with leaping and great joy.

When you know who praise is all about, then you can express yourself any way that the Bible, our praise handbook, allows. Find an opportunity this week to express praise in your body unto the Lord. Watch Him give victory, joy, and hope through your praise. Revolutionize your church by using the handbook on praising God.

Chapter 5

Creating An *Atmosphere*

When we first see the story of man and God in the book of Genesis, we see the story of praise and worship. Praise and worship are simply the means in which man communicates with God and God communicates with man. They are our fellowship with God and He with us. When we open the Bible and begin to read, we see that God was the first one who "created" the arena or atmosphere for communion. He created that utopian place called the Garden of Eden and placed man in it. Then each day He would descend into this atmosphere and spend time with Adam and Eve. He would share His thoughts and ways with them. He would probably listen to their issues and ideas. They would brag on each other and they would lean on each other during this time of fellowship.

God spent time developing this "perfect" place. He made it a place of purity (there was no sin). He made it a place of serenity (there was no violence). He made it a place of ministry (they were fed and cared for here). God was the first to create this atmosphere of fellowship.

But after man sinned and was driven out of the Garden in Genesis 3 it was no longer God's responsibility to create a place where He felt welcomed enough to come and commune with man. ***Now it became the responsibility of man to create the atmosphere for God.*** Before he allowed Adam and Eve to leave the Garden, God showed them exactly what it would take to create a place where He could fellowship with them again. In Genesis 3:21 the Bible tells us that God made Adam and Eve skins to clothe themselves and cover their nakedness (a sign of the sin that was now present in their bodies). The only way that God could have gotten these skins was to slay an animal and shed it's blood. The blood of the animal symbolically covered Adam and Eve's sinful nature, while the skin of the animal covered the physical representation of their sinful nature. God's plan was twofold to show them that redemption was possible and to show them that if they desired to commune with His holy presence again they would have to make sure they followed this example and created the right atmosphere where He could come down and dwell.

It was not long after they left the Garden that this was proven to be true. Cain and Able both brought offerings unto God. These children of Adam and Eve had obviously learned from their parents the plan that it took to create an atmosphere where God felt welcomed. For some reason Cain chose to ignore this plan and tried to get God to accept his plan instead. The Bible tells us that God chose not to come and dwell in the sacrifice of Cain. Abel created the right atmosphere by following the original plan of God and God had respect for that and descended to commune with Able. Creating the right atmosphere is key to getting God to show up.

Down through the Bible we see men who spent the proper time "creating" the atmosphere and then God in turn came down and blessed and honored their offerings. Elijah on Mt. Carmel spent much time preparing his altar. Digging round the base, pouring the water upon the sacrifice, praying for God to send His presence down and then it came. After Elijah created the right atmosphere then God came to fellowship with him.

The tabernacle in the wilderness was a great example of how man was now responsible for "creating" the atmosphere for God instead of the other way around. God gave Moses very detailed plans regarding this building where His presence would come and dwell. There were certain measurements, certain materials, certain workers, and certain processes that had to be used before His glory would come and dwell. In Exodus 29:43-46, God finishes his plans by telling Moses that if all this is done according to what He asks THEN He will come and dwell with the children of Israel. He makes is clear that creating the right atmosphere is the most important invitation you can issue to Him! In Exodus 40:33 the Bible tells us "then Moses finished all the work." He completed the process of creating the atmosphere and then Exodus 40:34-38 a cloud descends upon the tabernacle and the glory of God covers it. After man created the atmosphere the presence of God came and dwelt there and communed with man. But God could not come until man had created a place where He felt welcome.

A few years later, after the tabernacle had ceased to exit, Solomon created a new place for the presence of

God to dwell. In I Kings 8:1-13 we see that AFTER they had built the building, placed everything inside as it was supposed to be and offered the proper sacrifice that the presence of God descended upon that place. Throughout these examples the most important thing to note is that the presence of God DID NOT arrive until man had created Him an atmosphere.

Following Solomon's temple the Lord begins to establish a new dwelling place for His Spirit. Ezekiel 36:26-27 the Lord tells the prophet that there will come a day when He will place his Spirit inside of man instead of a tabernacle or a temple. Later on the prophet Joel prophesied in Joel 2:28 that one day God would pour out His Spirit upon all "flesh". Jesus shared even more of that plan with his disciples in John 14:17-20 when He told them that His dwelling place would now be "in them". He gave them even more insight in John 14:26 when he shared that he would send them the Comforter or The Holy Ghost who would dwell in them. In Acts 2:1-4 we see this unfold. But we have to understand that before the Holy Ghost filled their lives they spent 10 days preparing the atmosphere for this historic encounter. They had to create the place for His presence. I'm sure that time was filled with prayers of repentance, moments of unity, opportunities to heal breaches between themselves, sessions of singing and times of praise and worship before the sudden entrance of the Holy Ghost. They spent the proper time creating the atmosphere for His presence to feel welcome in that place. Only after they created the atmosphere did the Spirit appear and fill their lives with His presence. I Corinthians 3:16 tells us most emphatically that "we" are the temple of the Holy Ghost. To keep His Spirit welcome we need to make sure that we are always creating the right atmosphere. We need to keep our temple cleansed through the washing of the Word, the cleansing of our minds and hearts, the prayers of repentance, the communion of believers through right relationships, the uplifting of song, praise and worship unto God. If we do the right things to "create" the atmosphere then we don't have to worry about the presence of God dwelling with us.

How do we prepare ourselves? First of all we must be obedient to the voice of God. Moses listened and followed the plan of God. Abel followed the plan of God as given to him by his parents. Solomon did everything according to the plan laid out by God. The disciples tarried and waited on the presence of God according to the instruction of Jesus. Obedience always determines our relationship and connection with God. The more we obey, the more we can connect with God. In the Old Testament God had no respect for Saul's sacrifice because he wasn't obedient. In fact Samuel told Saul that obedience to God was more pleasing than his sacrifice. Obey the Word of God. Obey the plan of God and listen to the voice of God and you can create the right atmosphere for the presence of God.

Secondly follow the plan. So many people read the Word of God and yet they start making a few changes to the plan. We cannot do that and create the atmosphere where He is welcomed. Make sure that you understand the plan. The Bible asks you to be patient in tribulation – follow the plan. The Bible said you can leap for joy – then follow the plan. The Bible tells us to forgive and we will be forgiven – follow the plan. The Bible tells us to love one another even if we have been abused – follow the plan. The more you follow the plan the more you create an environment where the Spirit of the Lord feels welcome and will dwell.

So many people think they cannot obey without understanding all the answers. When my daughter was a baby she ran away from me in a parking lot. I told her (loudly and strongly) to stop but she didn't. When I reached her I gave her a spanking and told her never to do that again. She was too little to understand all the reasons why she shouldn't be allowed to run around in the parking lot. I couldn't explain to her understanding that she was small and drivers couldn't see her and they could back out and run over her. I couldn't help this child understand that she could be killed or hurt very badly. The only thing I could do is underline that when I speak you just have to obey sometimes without understanding all the reasoning behind it. There will be times when God can explain His plan to you but there will be others when He wants you to obey without understanding all the ins and outs. During those times you have to make sure that you obey knowing that He is your father and He would never ask anything of you that will hurt or damage you. Learn to obey the voice of God without hesitation and then you are one step closer to creating the right atmosphere for Him.

You have to have the right things in the house. The Lord was very specific with Moses regarding the make, materials, transportation and use of the instruments of worship in the tabernacle and temple. They had to be made exactly according to His plan, they had to be carried according to his plan and they had to be cared for and used according to His plan. Whenever they went around his plan (as when they tried to bring the ark of the covenant back to the temple the wrong way) there were always consequences. You have to make sure that you are placing the right things in your life and caring for them in the right manner. We cannot have the wrong things in our lives and expect the presence of God to descend upon us and minister to us through worship. We need to make sure that we are doing our best to keep the right things in our lives so that we can open the lines of communication with God.

Repentance is such an important part of creating the right atmosphere in our lives. I don't mind doing housework but my least favorite thing to do is dusting the furniture. But if I don't for a few days then I can write my name on it. The same is true of repentance. It is giving our lives a good dusting. We are polishing up all that furniture that we have placed in our lives and making sure that is clean for a visit from our Savior. I cannot expect God to visit my life and let His Shekinah glory in a dirty place. Utilize the tool of repentance. Keep a good supply of it in your life and make sure you use it on a regular basis. It should be a part of every day and every prayer that you pray. The cleaner we are, the more welcome the presence of God will be in our lives.

We need a right relationship with others to create the right atmosphere. Jesus told us that loving each other was the second greatest commandment. He showed us that if we could just simply grasp these two concepts that our lives would be a complete success. First we have to love God with all our hearts and then we have to love and treat each other as we would treat ourselves. Many churches don't experience true, open worship and fellowship with God during their services because they don't have right relationship with each other. Have you ever been invited to eat at someone's house? You got there and sat down at the table, but could tell that there was tension between the husband and his wife. It was most uncomfortable for you and you didn't want to be there. The same is true with God. He said everyone would know we are HIS disciples by how we love and treat each other. If you really want to create the right atmosphere then make your differences right the Biblically way.

In Matthew 18, Jesus gives us an entire chapter on how to make our difference right with each other. He talks to them about humility. He talks about being concerned if one of your brothers or sisters is lost. Then he tells us how to go and make an offence or a conflict right. Then we come to Matthew 18:18-20. These are scriptures that we love to preach and we love to talk about. But you have to understand that these verses are directly related to the verses before and after them. We cannot just pluck 18-20 out of the middle of Matthew 18 and expect them to come to pass. Immediately following these scriptures Jesus talks about how much and how often we are to forgive one another. I believe that we can experience Matthew 18:18 and the power to bind and loose on earth and in heaven IF we have been obedient to making our relationship with our brothers and sisters right first and forgiving one another. I know that I can receive Matthew 18:19 about agreeing together as touching "anything" and it will be done for me but only IF I have been obedient to the rest of Matthew 18. I am glad that I can come to church and see Matthew 18:20, about 2 or 3 of us gathering together in His name and He will show up, coming to pass but only IF I have made sure I have followed through with the rest of Matthew 18. A huge part of creating the atmosphere for God in our services is to make sure that our relationship with our brothers and sisters is Biblically correct.

If we are careful about doing our part in creating the atmosphere we won't have to worry about the presence of God moving our services! He will show up when we create the atmosphere.

Chapter 6

Making The *Connection*

Matthew 18:20 lets us know that if just two or three of us meet in His name that He is there. When we create the right atmosphere, then the problem is never that God isn't there and ready to bless, heal, save, and set free. The problem is that we don't connect with Him. We have to be careful not to allow things to hinder our connection to God. God is always there to meet our needs. He is always there ready to help us overcome our situations. The question is, are we really there?

Many people come to church hoping God just takes attendance. They come hoping that by showing up they will get a star by their name. You may get noticed for being at church, but you get answers in praise. I don't believe that God only takes attendance; I believe God wants students who are involved in the process of learning of Him. He wants to see praise on their lips, a shout in their voice, dancing and leaping, clapping and singing unto Him.

When my daughter, Caitlin began school, I also started back to school. However, I quickly learned that God did not give me the talent to be a schoolteacher. I enjoy dropping my daughter off at school and knowing someone else has to spend that time helping her learn things. When we do homework together, we often butt heads. I want her to enjoy learning, to be excited to do her homework, and to get it over with so that she can move on to other things. She wants to move on to other things right away, and so we have this very contentious setting. I began to realize that if I would go through her homework and praise her for the good grades she received, if we would talk a little about the good things that she had done that day, or if we started with the subjects that she enjoyed, her homework got done the right way quickly. God often waits for us to praise Him for what He has done before He helps us with the hard stuff. We want Him to fix everything that's not right, solve all the difficult problems, and make the hard things go away first.

Prayer before service is essential to the praiser! It is the opportunity to let go of carnality, cleanse your mind, renew your spirit, and make your heart ready to receive. But praise is when you connect, or plug in, to the activating power of God. Prayer is a chance to get your spirit right, and praise is an opportunity to get everything else right.

I enjoy all the benefits of electricity. Growing up the Philippines, I really enjoyed my air conditioner, cold drinks from the refrigerator and lights to see by. Living in Manila, we experienced what were called "brown-outs." These were not full blackouts, where the whole city went dark. Brownouts were where a certain area of town would lose electricity. I can remember during many brownouts, when the heat became unbearable, getting out of bed and lying on the marble floor to cool off. If you were using the computer for any reason, you always stopped every few minutes to save your material, just in case of a brownout. We don't realize how much we need electricity to run our lives until it's gone. Have you ever tried to use a cordless phone without electricity, check your email, get cool air or heat, run any device such as a tape or video player, or even the small things like dry your hair or plug in your curlers? We have become so dependent on electricity that it's only when we don't have it that we understand its importance in our lives.

I've also found that if you have electricity, you still need a good connection to get the maximum benefit from it. We used to live in a home where the electricity ran from the pole to our house above ground. The slightest high wind would cause it to disconnect, and then we would have to wait for the electric company to come out and reattach the line.

Praise and worship is our connection to God. It plugs us into His Spirit that is already present in our midst. It is the electricity that activates what we need in our lives. You have to plug your spirit into the Spirit of God through praise and worship. *So many people are standing there, holding the cord, needing the benefits of God in their lives, but they won't plug into it.* Praise and worship is an individual responsibility. I would love to be able to plug in for you, but I cannot. God created you to praise Him in your own, unique way. It is your outlet to God, so why do you stand there when all you need to do is connect?

When you begin to praise God, then you actually open the connection between Him and you. The juice is turned on and there becomes a flow between your spirit and His Spirit. Paul told Timothy to "stir up" the gift that was in him (II Timothy 1:6). Praise begins to stir up the gift of the Holy Ghost. It activates that power in your life. You need the power of God moving on your situation, you need the Holy Ghost strengthening your life, and you need God to answer your request and needs. Plug into the power! Over and over again throughout the Bible the Lord said these words, "He that hath an ear, let him hear what the Spirit is saying." Praise and worship gets our spiritual ear listening to the voice of God. You need that power and that connection in your life.

When you enter your service this week, ask yourself this question, "Am I connected to God?" Don't just show up to get a check mark beside your name; show up to get the answers to your situation through praise.

Chapter 7

Just *The Tool*

As I said in chapter 1 of this book, inanimate objects are simply the *tools* of worship. Instruments and music are not worship within themselves. They are only the tools that let us know it's our time to worship. Remember, they blew the horns at Jericho every day but the victory was not won until the people shouted. The horns were simply the call to worship.

Music in our churches today is simply the *blowing of the horns* that it is time for us, the people, to rise up and worship. When we sit on the pew, silently and without any participation, we are using our music as a crutch. We are trying to convince ourselves, and God, that it *is our* worship. We want it to be our prosthetics and walk for us, or perhaps our wheelchair. We say we will just sit in them and they can move us around. But a wheelchair doesn't move without some human effort involved. It needs a living being to turn the wheels, or push the handles, or move the lever for it to make any movement. And where there is no movement, there is no progress. Music, instruments and the playing of them is simply the call to **THE PEOPLE** to step up and get the job done. But these instruments **cannot** worship for you! Remember in Psalms 150 David told us over and over again that we praise *with* all these instruments and we praise God *upon* them. However, these items by themselves, and without human touch, cannot utter one sound of praise or worship unto God.

And each week in churches around the world, the call goes forth and the people do not answer. At the first note played and the first word sung, the call goes forth. But so many people just sit and observe this taking place. They sit in their situations, their needs and their sickness and never take advantage of the call to defeat the enemy of their lives. Music is the call but worship is *YOUR WEAPON!* A weapon is useless unless you pick it up and use it. Unless you pick up worship as your weapon, you will never defeat anything in your life.

And then people blame the "tool" for their lack of connection. They give excuses about the music being too loud, too contemporary, too old-fashioned and out-of-date. They didn't like the singer, they didn't like the soloist, or they were upset because they didn't get the solo. And on and on it goes until I'm sure God is sick of hearing our excuses instead of our worship.

When you go to build a shelf and it comes out crooked, does the carpenter blame the tool? No! The first thing he will do is look to himself. The hammer didn't pick itself up and build the shelf incorrect. The level didn't determine if the bubble was in the middle. The saw didn't cut the wrong length of wood. The measuring tape didn't determine the wrong measurements. A carpenter realizes that if the shelf failed to be built correctly, the blame lies with him. Why then, do we blame the music for our lack of connection to God? Music can never be our connection to God it is *our call* ***to connect***. But if we don't answer the call it wasn't because we didn't hear it ring. It was because we chose to press ignore.

Music is simply the call. It is the alarm going off in your home saying it's time to get up and defend yourself. It is the open sign in the window that tells you the doctor is in the office and open for appointments. It is the whistle at the start of the race that says, GO! GO! GO! It is the trumpets announcing that the King is on the throne and ready for an audience with you. But if we see and hear the call and do not answer, then we are the issue and not the tool.

To compensate for our lack of participation, churches have tried to wake us up and get our attention. They have put up cool lighting and flashing lights, creating a nightclub affect. They tell themselves if we do this then surely people will get up and respond like they do in the nightclubs. But they don't! Or we put words on the screen with moving scenes behind them to create the effect that we are watching TV or at the movies to get people to respond. But they don't! Or we arrange ourselves like a "real" band with guitars out front and other instruments behind so that perhaps the people will feel they are at a concert and connect and respond. But they don't! Or we modulate, add complicated orchestration, or a special drum loop to make them feel they are at a symphony or a big event to get them to respond. But they don't! In fact some of these things have created even more disconnect with the people. Don't misunderstand me, any of this can be added and it is not wrong. However, if we are using this to compensate for the lack of worship on the part of the people, these things will NEVER produce that! All these things are inanimate objects and tools to announce the call to worship. True worship can only come from the people! Instead of changing all these things, let's first start working on changing the people. Because when the people respond, all the rest fades into the background. God is not looking at those things to produce worship, but His eyes are always looking to the people to step up. All God needs is your voice, your hands, your feet and your sincere heart to find a personal connection with you.

Chapter 8

The *Difference in Praise & Worship*

To really participate in praise and worship the way that we need to, we have to understand the differences between the two. Often when exhorting the saints, we will use these two words as interchangeable. However, they are not the same thing. They describe two different ways of connecting to God.

Praise is an action word. *Vine's Expository Dictionary* describes this word in Hebrew as "halal," meaning to celebrate, glory, or boast about. It signified a certain type of shouting or jubilation. When a king would step out in front of a large crowd he would be greeted by "halal" praise, a large roar of approval, a boasting that this was a special person, a celebration of the person in the position. Psalms 113-118 are referred to as the "Hallel Psalms" because they boast of the God who delivered the children of Israel from Egypt by the hand of Moses. The word "halal" is also the root of the word Hallelujah. In fact, "hallelujah" translated means, "Praise the LORD." "Hallel" means to praise and "jah" is another form of the word "Yah" which is the root of Yahweh or Jehovah. So when you say "Hallelujah!" you are praising God for being your Savior and King!

Remember that we praise God for who He is. The word hallelujah means to praise Jehovah. Throughout the Old Testament before God revealed His name, Jesus, He was referred to as YHWH, Yahweh or Jehovah. Because God wasn't ready to reveal the fullness of His name, Jesus, He revealed Himself in different ways. He called Himself Jehovah and then He revealed Himself through acts that He performed.

When Abraham needed a sacrifice on Mount Moriah to take the place of Isaac, God revealed Himself as Jehovah-Jireh, or God the Provider.
When Israel sinned against God and needed divine healing, God had Moses erect the golden rod with the snake. When they looked upon it, they were healed. In this act, God revealed Himself as Jehovah-Rapha, or God the Healer.

When Israel needed victory in battle as Aaron and Hur held up the hands of Moses, God came through for them and revealed Himself as Jehovah-Nissi, or God our Banner. (The word banner is used because of the way warfare used to be fought. Each army would have a banner representing their country or their lord. Everyone fighting would always look for the banner. As long as the banner was still flying, they were winning the war. When they could no longer see the banner, they knew that their side had been defeated. That was why it was so important for the banner to remain flying.)

Other revelation names for Jehovah are: Jehovah-m'kaddesh, God our Sanctification; Jehovah-shalom, God our Peace; Jehovah-sabaoth, God of Hosts (almighty); Jehovah-elyon, God most High; Jehovah-raah, God my Shepherd; Jehovah-hoseenu, God our Maker; Jehovah-tsidkenu, God our Righteousness; and Jehovah-shammah, God who is present. The next time you shout "Hallelujah," realize that you are praising Jehovah. Then remember all the things that He has done for you and praise Him according to His acts. If He has healed you, praise Him for being Jehovah-Rapha! If he has delivered you, praise Him for being Jehovah-Nissi! When you say "Hallelujah," you say more than just a praise word. You actually praise God for all His wonderful characteristics.

Praise is a very active word. When you use praise, you are using an outward form to express the worthiness of the person you are lauding. That is why even creation can praise God. The sun, moon, stars, trees, and all creation praise God by continuing to remain in the order in which He created them according to Psalm 8:3. Creation praises God by its very existence.

In the Old Testament, there are different words that are used to express types of praise unto God.

Yadah (yaw-dah): to worship with an extended hand; the giving of oneself in worship and adoration; to lift your hand unto the Lord. It is seen in the act of a small child surrendering and asking their parent to 'pick them up and carry them'. It is found in Genesis 29:35, 2 Chronicles 7:6 and Psalm 9:1 which says, *"I will praise thee, O LORD, with my whole heart; I will shew forth all thy marvellous works."*

Towday (to-daw): to worship with an extended hand; not as an act of surrender, but as an act of agreeing regarding what has been done or will be done. Thanking God for something you don't have in the natural yet. There is great faith in Towdah praise. You are praising simply because you *know* God's Word is *true!* It is found in Psalm 42:4, Jeremiah 17:26 and Psalm 50:23 which says, *"Whoso offereth praise glorifieth me: and to him that ordereth his conversation aright will I shew the salvation of God."*

Tehillah (teh-hi-law): to sing straight to God; a *spontaneous* new song; singing from a melody in your heart. This is an unrehearsed, unprepared song. It brings about a unity to the church. One can move into tehillah praise at any point but once the melody has been sung once, the praise will then become zamar praise. It is found in Psalm 22:3, 2 Chronicles 20:22 and Psalm 34:1 which says, *"I will bless the LORD at all times: his praise shall continually be in my mouth."* We find a great example of this in Exodus 15:1-19 when Moses begins to spontaneously praise God for the delivering them from the Egyptians.

Zamar (zah-mar): prepared singing; to sing with instruments. The word zamar means to touch the strings, this includes the instrumental worship found in Psalm 150. Psalm 92:1, *"It is a good thing to give thanks unto the LORD, and to sing praises unto thy name, O Most High:"* This takes place in Exodus 15:20-21 when Miriam picks up the tambourine and takes over the song of Moses.

Barak (bah-rak): to kneel or bow; there is a sense of kneeling and blessing God as an act of adoration. To kneel as you would before a King or ruler. You are yielding to the fact that He is royalty and worthy of your humility. We find examples of this in Genesis 24:48 and

56

Romans 14:11 which says, *"For it is written, As I live, saith the Lord, every knee shall bow to me, and every tongue shall confess to God.".*

Halel (haw-lal): to be clear, to shine; to make a show, to boast in the Lord; to rave. This type of praise is exuberant and often can appear foolish to those looking at it. It involves running, dancing, leaping, jumping, clapping and shouting. David showcased this type of worship when the ark was returning to Jerusalem in 2 Samuel 6:12-16 and 21-23. We also see this played out in Psalm 113-119, as referenced above, when David gives praise to God for the entire history of His blessings and deliverance upon Israel.

Shabach (shaw-bakh): to address in a loud tone, loud adoration, a shout; to proclaim. It is a testimony of praise. It is not just about being loud, but it is also about being uninhibited and placing your whole heart, soul, mind and body into praising God. We see this in Joshua 6:5, 10, 20 when the children of Israel take down the city of Jericho. And then again in Ezra 3:10-13 when the foundation of the temple is laid allowing it to be rebuilt in Jerusalem. Ezra 3:12-13, *"But many of the priests and Levites and chief of the fathers, who were ancient men, that had seen the first house, when the foundation of this house was laid before their eyes, wept with a loud voice; and many shouted aloud for joy: So that the people could not discern the noise of the shout of joy from the noise of the weeping of the people: for the people shouted with a loud shout, and the noise was heard afar off."*

The word worship is a smaller, more intimate word. It was used to describe someone who was actually allowed into the throne room with the king. This person wasn't seeing the king at a distance (as the praise word denotes) but actually having a face-to-face talk with him. It is the word used in translation regarding Esther's approach into the throne room. She actually bowed or prostrated herself before the king who then in turn gave her a personal audience. He listened to her alone and responded to her request.

Worship is a more intimate act than praise. It is actually being singled out of the praise crowd for a one-on-one talk with the King! When you enter worship, you actually walk into a different room with God and have an intimate conversation with Him. Worship is where you can connect heart-to-heart with God. His presence is there to hear and respond to your request.

Worship is always pretty. The picture of worship in the Bible is a father standing over his son with a knife clutched in his upraised hand; it's an unselfish woman offering everything she has to the possible death of her own family; it is a high man name Joseph being able to humble himself and forgive those who has so terribly wronged him. Praise is connected with thanksgiving and exaltation, but worship is connected to sacrifice.

Worship comes from a different place in our spirits and it is reserved for God alone (Luke 4:8). It is the art of losing ourselves in the complete adoration of another. Worship is intertwined with complete surrender of self and complete awareness of God.

The tabernacle of the Old Testament was a physical representation of this spiritual concept of praise and worship. The outer courts were accessible to ordinary Israelites. They brought their sacrifices to the door of the Tabernacle where it had to be offered for their sins. They could approach the outer courts, but the inner courts were for the priests only. Only a member of the tribe of Levi was allowed into this inner sanctum. And it was only the high priest, Aaron, who could enter the Holy of Holies once a year. It was very difficult to enter into the place where the presence of the Lord dwelt upon the Ark of the Covenant. But when Jesus died on Calvary and the curtain was torn in half, all humanity was given permission to come directly into His presence. Hebrews 4:16 tells us that now we can boldly approach the throne of grace. If we truly want an audience with King, then we have within ourselves the ability to be chosen for that meeting.

Each government and kingdom of the world has a department, which oversees protocol. Protocol deals with every aspect of having a meeting with the president, prime minister, king or queen of a country. There are certain demands made of anyone who wishes to meet these people face to face. The protocol department makes sure that each visitor knows exactly what needs to be done to ensure the proper respect is given for the position the leader holds. When meeting the Queen of England there are certain ways that you must shake hands, bow or curtsy, and even address her. The same thing goes with the President of the United States. Each country of the world has an entire department devoted to making sure each person is given the praise and respect they are due. How much more should we endeavor to make sure we can have a meeting with the King of Kings and Lord of Lords? How much more should we desire to be in His presence, worshipping Him? To achieve that, we must make sure that we have been selected to enter the throne room and have a meeting with God! Remember if you are a member of the praise and worship team at your church, then you are a member of God's protocol team and your job is teach others how to properly respect, love and approach the King of Kings!

The unique thing about praise and worship is they are a one-two tag team. You really can't have one without the other. Praise is the beginning, and worship is the end! You start in one and end up in the other. I like to think of it like this: Praise is the avenue, but worship is the destination. When I begin in praise, then God can pick me from the crowd and invite me into the throne room for an intimate talk with Him.

The format for prayer given by Jesus in the New Testament also agrees with this. In what is known as "The Lord's Prayer," Jesus taught His disciples to pray by praising first before entering a place where they could make personal requests. He then ended the prayer with praise also. Matthew 6:9-13 shows us that we praise, we worship (or present our request one-on-one before God), and then we end with praise and thanksgiving again.

Praise is the physical response to the presence of God, but worship is the spiritual connection. In the chapter entitled, "Who Is It All About?" I address the activeness of praise. Praise is taking your physical body and forcing it to respond to God. It is singing, clapping, dancing, shouting, leaping, and showing God through a physical response your adoration and admiration for Him. When you praise, you are standing together with many others boasting about your God! Praise is a time to bring our carnal flesh under submission to the spiritual man. We use this sinful body that has been redeemed to show forth the praises of God. Often the greatest obstacle to a great praise service is the flesh of men. To enter into praise you have to force your flesh to respond. Praise and worship leaders spend a great amount of their time trying to get people to respond in the flesh so that their spirit can enter into worship. God responds to the person who responds to Him. Abraham took Isaac all the way to Mount Moriah, tied him up, and raised the knife before God intervened with an answer. Even Elijah built an altar with 12 stones, dug a trench around it, put on the wood, and poured on the water before the fire fell from heaven. The children of Israel marched 13 times around the walls of Jericho and shouted before the walls fell flat. Even in the New Testament Jesus walked by many people who were sick, but He healed the ones who cried out to Him for help. Blind Bartimaeus cried out to Jesus as He was passing by. His action produced a reaction by God! Paul and Silas "sang praises" to God before the earthquake took place. Your praise action will produce a reaction in the heart of God. He reacts to your action! Many people never enter into worship because they never get His attention through praise. If inanimate objects can praise God by simply existing, the only thing we need to praise God is breath. Psalm 150:6 commands, *"Let everything that hath **BREATH** praise the Lord. Praise ye the Lord!"* If you are breathing, then you are able to praise the Lord.

Once you make that physical response of praise, then a spiritual connection begins to take place. This is where you actually enter into worship. This is where the outward response becomes an inward emotional connection to God! He invites you into His presence for an intimate talk. Praise and worship leader, if you can ever build your service to the point where people can enter this realm this is where needs are truly met without a lot of other interference. People get lost at this point in worshipping God. Tears flow, people fall on their faces in the altar, there's groaning and weeping before God!

We can even see the difference through the tool of music. I often strive to start our services with what I call praise music. Faster, upbeat music and songs that proclaim the goodness of God--songs in which people can clap, leap, and shout unto God. But as I feel that breakthrough take place, I may change the mood of the service by slowing down the music, using songs that talk about how much I love God, how wonderful He has been to me, how much I trust Him. I turn to songs that express a more intimate relationship with God.

With praise, the only requirement for humans is breath; with worship the only requirement is spirit and truth. John 4:24 states, *"God is a Spirit: and they that worship Him must worship Him in spirit and in truth."* Worship happens when we get a chance to really know who He is in the fullness of truth. We become on intimate terms with the Lord. We enter a new dimension of relationship with God!

Everyone knows who the President of the United States is, but few people are known by the President. It's one thing to say that you know the Lord, but it's another for Him to recognize you. I love the story found in Matthew 16:13-19. Jesus asked the disciples a question: *"Who do men say that I the Son of Man am?"* Suddenly the disciples start sharing what others are saying about His identity, but Jesus then makes it more personal by asking, *"But whom say ye that I am?"* Or, I don't really care about everyone else right now. I'm interested in seeing if you really know Me. Of course that wonderful, impetuous Peter jumps in with the answer, *"Thou are the Christ, the Son of the Living God."* For all the times that Peter got the wrong answer, this was the time when he got it all right. He identified Jesus not only as a great teacher or prophet but as the prophesied Messiah when he said, "the Christ." He confirmed that he understood that Jesus wasn't just a great man, but He was the living flesh of the eternal God! But the beautiful part of this story is that after Peter recognized who Jesus was, Jesus made a statement to Peter. In verse 18 he says, *"Thou art Peter!"* All the sudden, the King knew Peter by name; he recognized him in a unique and special way. And not only did Jesus recognize Peter, but He gave him some things for the future. Don't get caught up in the lie that just because you go to church that's all you need to do to be recognized by God. In Matthew 7:21-27 Jesus shares some insight into being known by Him. He says that just because you know all the right things to do doesn't mean that He will recognize you. Verse 23 says that in the day that our works are judged, He will say to some, *"Depart from me, I NEVER KNEW YOU!"* He is looking for someone to activate the Word, to praise Him, to really know Him as their Savior, to really understand who He is and why He came. When you can do those things you will have an audience with the King, and not only will you know Him but He will truly know you.

I believe that with more understanding of the differences between praise and worship, we can enhance our worship services. My responsibility as a praise and worship leader is to lead God's people down the avenue of praise and try to help them enter the arena of worship. Everyone needs to be encouraged to activate the fleshly body in praise and then get a personal invitation into the throne room for a one-on-one talk with God!

Chapter 9

Praising *Through The Test*

Praise is the key element when you are going through a time of testing in God. If you don't learn to praise THROUGH the test instead of after the test, you may have to repeat the test to get the right results.

To really understand this we must understand the process of testing. Webster's Dictionary defines a test as "a critical examination or evaluation." Another word for test is trial and that is defined as "an experiment to test quality, value or usefulness." The definition alone helps us understand that this won't be a time of pleasure, but a time of pressure.

Even the use of the word critical lets us know that this could be a matter of life or death. When something is critical, it's of the most importance to the future. When someone is placed in the Intensive Care Unit (ICU) in the hospital, they are in critical care. They are in a protected environment where they can be monitored for signs of progress 24 hours a day. The nurses at the desk are always watching their vital signs for any negative development. Not only are they watched by the nurses, but visitors cannot enter the room without prior approval. They are protected from others as well.

When God takes you through a time of test or trial, He puts you in Heaven's ICU. But I love the fact that He doesn't just allow anyone access to you. The devil cannot just approach your life during a time of testing from God and do whatever he wants. When Job was being tested, Satan could not come against him without prior approval from God. He had to approach the throne of God each time he wanted to do something to Job.

Testing is a critical time in a person's life, and what that person does during this time can alter the outcome.

Most items that you purchase have been put through a trial or test. They have been placed under strenuous circumstances to prove that they are made with quality. The better the items perform during the test the more value they are given. If an item fails a trial, then the creators of the item go back to the drawing board, remake the item and then place it back under the trial for new results. I'm sure the three Hebrew boys were glad that they passed their test the first time. That wasn't a test they would have wanted to take again. I know Abraham could sigh with relief that he had passed the test the Lord demanded concerning Isaac at Mount Moriah.

We have to understand that trials are a part of our life to refine us as silver or gold (Jeremiah 9:7, Daniel 11:35, and Zechariah 13:9), but we can determine the outcome by our actions during the test.

Knowing that we will all be tested, we need to understand that there are three ways a test can come to us.

66

First of all, there's "God's tests." These are times that God puts us in the fire to determine our quality, value, and usefulness to His Kingdom. Jonah had a test from God. The Lord had given him a job to do, but Jonah thought he knew better for his life. Jonah could not refuse to take the test and walk away. When God has a test for you, just go ahead and do what He desires for you to do. Jonah's test took him all the way to the belly of the whale. It wasn't until Jonah began to praise God that his circumstances changed. In Jonah chapter 2 he's in the belly of the whale crying out to God. In verses 1-8, all Jonah can do is cry and complain about his circumstances. It isn't until verse 9 that his prayer changes to praise. He says, "But I will sacrifice unto thee with the voice of thanksgiving, I will pay that that I have vowed. Salvation is of the Lord." The instant he utters these words of praise the fish spits him out on dry ground. Praise was what changed the circumstances in Jonah's test from God. Complaining during a test will never help you pass the test. In fact, complaining will turn God's ear from you. He is interested in praise, not complaints! Always remember that God's test for us is intended to bring out the good in our lives.

The second kind of test is Satan's test. The good news is that if you are a child of God, Satan cannot test you without the permission of your Father. He must ask for the chance to come against you. In Job chapter 1 we see that Satan had to appear before God and ask permission to attack Job. Even then, God put restrictions and limits on Satan. There were things he was allowed to do, but there were things he wasn't allowed to do. Each time Satan wanted to *"up the ante"*, so to speak, he had to appear and get permission from God. The quickest way through Satan's test is to understand your power in God. The Lord has given us many ways to get through a test from Satan. Satan fears the Word, the Name, the Blood, and the Holy Ghost, and he cannot stand before the simple resistance of a believer. When you praise the Name of Jesus and resist the devil, he is powerless to continue his attack against you. Job never cursed God, nor did he ever cease to trust in God to help him. How defeated Satan must have felt when Job said, *"Though He slay me, yet will I trust Him."* (Job 13:15) Satan's tests are the easiest to pass. Don't allow them to come against your life over and over again.

When I was a child, I greatly feared Halloween. I didn't like the masks, and I didn't appreciate all the images that went with the holiday. My brother, Marty, is two years older than me and when he realized the fear he could instill in me by wearing a scary mask and jumping out from behind the furniture, my life became a nightmare. My father, who was a very wise man, took me off to the side and gave me sage advice. He instructed me that if I didn't jump and scream every time Marty tried to scare me that it wouldn't be as much fun for him to scare me. So the next time he jumped out and tried to scare me, I stood my ground. I was shaking in my boots, but I didn't allow myself to scream and run. After a few times of that my brother realized that he couldn't scare me and so he gave up and went out to scare the neighborhood children.

So many Christians run screaming and crying every time the devil says "Boo!" that they spend their whole walk with God running from situation to situation. If they could just learn to stand their ground and let Satan know that his attack is never going to succeed, then the devil would give up and go look for easier prey. I love that the Bible tells us that we don't have to fight the devil; all we have to do is resist the devil. Resistance is not pushing forward but simply holding your ground! Stand your ground and watch Satan run for a change!

The third test that we can endure is our test. Many times because of doubt, unbelief, and disobedience, we go through a test in our lives. We remove ourselves from the protective umbrella of God's hand and then we are exposed to the rain. We know that we will all go through things in our lives because the Bible tells us that it rains on the just and the unjust (Matthew 5:45). God is as bound by His Word as you and I, and things that have been written in His Word will come to pass. He cannot remove that scripture concerning the rain in our lives, but I know that's why He placed other scriptures as our umbrella scriptures. Romans 8:28 gives us an umbrella during the rain by letting us know that even though things happen in our lives it is all working together for our good! But many times through our own actions, we take ourselves out from under the umbrella of God and expose ourselves to the elements. King David did this when he chose to sin with Bathsheba and then conspired with Joab to murder Bathsheba's husband. When David did this he put himself through a test. It wasn't God or Satan coming against him; it was David's own actions that produced a test in his life. Because of his actions, he lost his first child with Bathsheba and endured the rebuke of the prophet Nathan. When David repented and turned back to God in praise, the circumstances in his life changed. Be careful that you are not putting yourself through a test and then trying to ask God to explain why He is testing you.

No matter the test, it is always our reaction that determines our result. It is not the response afterwards that counts, but the response during the test that matters.

Being a missionary kid I went through every type of schooling there is. I went to public school, private school, and home school. The ACE program was one curriculum I had in my education. The problem with ACE is that if you don't have someone watching you, it is easy to get the answers to the test before you take it. When you know the answers beforehand, it's easy to pass the test. But in most tests, you don't get the answers ahead of time. Unless you study and get prepared, you won't pass the test. So many times when I've gotten a test back, I've looked over it and gotten upset with myself because I knew the answers to the questions I got wrong. But never have I been able to go to the teacher and say, "I really did know the correct answer to this question, so will you give me credit for it?" So far I've been unlucky in getting the grade changed. The important time is when you are taking the test. That is when knowing the right answers pays off!

The answer is always found in praise. When we use praise during our test, we show God that we are filled with faith.

In Genesis 22 we read the story of Abraham and Isaac going to Mount Moriah. When God asked this hard thing of Abraham, Abraham never questioned God. In fact, he just began to get everything ready. He got his servants, his donkeys, his wood, the knife and Isaac and began the journey. Abraham didn't understand the test, but he did understand the importance of praise and worship. Genesis 22:5 gives us insight into his attitude concerning this event: *"And Abraham said unto his young men, 'Abide ye here with the ass; and I and the lad will go yonder and WORSHP, and come again to you."* Abraham knew what the Lord had asked him to do to Isaac on Mount Moriah, yet he told his servants that he and Isaac's purpose for going to the mountain was to worship God! His attitude was one of praise unto the Lord. Because of his praise the Lord provided the sacrifice and found a great trust relationship with Abraham.

Praise has the power to transform any situation in your life. Acts 16 describes Paul and Silas beaten, bruised, chained, and sitting in the darkness. They were waiting for the sun to rise and their death sentence to be given. The Bible says in Acts 16:25 that "at midnight," they reacted to this terrible, seemingly hopeless situation. They sang praises unto God! Paul and Silas' reaction was to begin to praise God, and God's result was an earthquake that set them free and even produced salvation for others around them.

When you are in a situation that seems hopeless, why don't you try praise? Not only were Paul and Silas freed, but all those imprisoned with them were also set free. Your freedom from your circumstance through praise could be the key for someone else going through a test to be free also! Your praise could produce a domino effect in the lives of others around you.

The most wonderful thing about taking a test is when it is over. When you know you've done your best and now you can just wait for the results. Webster's Dictionary defines the word "tried" as "to be found trustworthy through testing." You see, when you have been tried (a past-tense experience), then you have passed the test with flying colors. You can now move on to bigger and better things. Job understood this concept. In Job 23:10 he said, *"But he knoweth the way that I take: when he hath tried me, I shall come forth as gold."* Job knew that if he could pass the test, then he would be found as gold in the sight of God. It takes a lot of fire and intense heat to take a lump of dirty earth and transform it into gold. But when you see the finished product, its beauty, value, and usefulness is immeasurable.

Don't allow your circumstances to control you; create a reaction that will produce heavenly results. Make a decision now, before the test begins, that when your time of trial comes you will go through it with praise. When things are the darkest in your life, you will lift up your voice in praise and worship. When God's request doesn't seem to make sense to you, you will still continue your walk with praise. My philosophy has always been that when I feel the test coming, I immediately start praising God. I want my time of testing to be as short as possible, and I want to learn my lesson right the first time. Praise is my avenue through my test. Let praise lift you out of your time of testing!

Chapter 10

Inspiration *or Desperation?*

This chapter is for praise and worship leaders. I believe that many churches are missing opportunity after opportunity to create this atmosphere of praise and lead the people into a place of worship. I think we have it all wrong because we believe that we have been hired to be "music" ministers. We think our job is only about getting the chords right, learning the newest or latest song, teaching the parts and then putting it all together on a Sunday. We feel if we have done that then we have "done our job." I strongly disagree, because what our people need is not more music. Pentecost has the greatest musicians, singers and performers of any denomination, but that is not fulfilling the purpose of music according to the Bible. Don't get me wrong, I'm all for doing your best, practicing and giving your best, but I don't want it to be about my performance. I want it to be about leading people into the place where they have a connection with God.

Instead of calling myself the Music Minister of The Turning Point, I am called the Worship Pastor. My job is as a shepherd of worship among our congregation. I want to keep my job description always before me. My responsibility is to create an atmosphere where people can be led into the throne room. Before each service my musicians and singers meet to pray. Our prayer is that we would be vessels of praise that God's anointing can flow through. Our desire is that through our talents a door would be opened into the presence of Almighty God. We yield our abilities to the hand of God for His leading and pray for His mind during the service.

I go many places and hear many great and talented individuals. But often I leave a service frustrated by the lack of opportunity to actually praise and worship God. I feel as though I am often being entertained by good singers who don't really understand their purpose. They have beautiful voices and choose wonderful songs, but they are simply performing to the crowd. If I pay money to go to a concert that is what I expect to hear, but when I go to church I am going for a different reason. They have been given an opportunity to create an atmosphere of praise but often they miss their purpose.

The other side of this issue is the frustration of a worship leader. When I do create the opportunity and the atmosphere and people do not take advantage of it, I can feel frustrated and then allow that to show. Knowing the needs of the people, understanding that their answers can be found in praise and worship, and yet seeing them not respond can produce a frustration in me that is then relayed to the congregation. There have been times when I have been harsh with a congregation while trying to promote worship. I try to force or make them praise and worship. I quickly learned that this was not effective. In fact, it would only frustrate me and the people more. I had to learn that my responsibility was to choose the right song, sing to the best of my ability, lead through my own praise and worship and trust that those who desired it would follow. I try to be positive and use scripture to produce faith.

One thing that we have recently instituted in our church is the concept that we *worship* **before** we worship! I know crazy concept right?! But remember David told us in Psalm 150 that the instruments do not praise God but we, the people, praise Him on and with the instruments. The truth is that the first instruments every created were US!! Our vocal chords for tone and pitch, our united vocal singing for harmony and parts and our hands and feet for rhythm and beat! We are the first instrument that needs to tune up and get ready for the service. So before we being to play and sing the first note, we take a few minutes and simply lift our hands, open our mouths and begin to praise God. Our worship leader will not preach to the people, but instead will worship God in the microphone to lead the people in how to participate in this. Our worship team will lift their hands, clap, shout unto God and exalt Him. This moment can last for a few moments or several minutes depending on if we feel the people have truly participated and begin to connect to God through worship. After we started this, we begin to notice an immediate change in our worship services. Where before it took so much longer for people to plug into and connect with God, that time was shortened. They seem to find a place of deeper worship in a shorter amount of time. It brings their mind into the sanctuary. It gives them an opportunity to lay aside all the weights and distractions and simply focus on their responsibility to the presence of God. It is one of the greatest things we have done in to promote and connect in worship in our church!

We don't have to strictly rely on music and singing. In fact, the Bible gives us this example in Psalms. Throughout this book we see the word, "Selah." This word means praise break. The singers would stop singing and would actually take a praise break. I often use this in my worship services. After we have sung for a while then the musicians will play, but I will instruct the people to take a praise break. This has been extremely effective in our church. Many times it has taken over the service as a new level of praise and worship will break out. I encourage you to try this in your next worship service and watch your people break forth in praise.

It is vitally important for a worship leader to promote worship through inspiration and not desperation. When I have tried through desperation to make people praise, it only produced frustration for me and them. So my responsibility is to read the Bible, pray and when I lead in worship share my inspiration from the Word of God. The thoughts of this book that I have received through inspiration, I have also shared with the congregation. When a worship leader tries to direct the people from a spirit of desperation they will find they create frustration.

When Saul tried to hold onto the rule of Israel through desperation, it became his ultimate downfall. God had removed His anointing from Saul and placed it upon David (a true worshipper). Yet because Saul could not accept this he tried through every desperate means to hold onto the kingdom. To hold onto the anointing, he even went so far as to chase David through mountains and caves to try to kill him. Instead of running towards God in repentance and coming back into right relationship with God, he chased after David to destroy him.

Worship leaders MUST keep themselves committed, dedicated and consecrated to God. Our inspiration to lead in worship is found through our anointing and our anointing is released through consecration. Worship leaders should be at prayer meetings, in Bible Study, sitting in church hearing the Word of God, and in the altar. If they are not, then they are just Music Directors and not Worship Leaders.

Chapter 11

The Game *or The Goal?*

So many times we get so involved in the game that we forget the goal. I have seen teams that played a perfect game but lost it all because they were so technically correct but they could never score. Then I have seen teams that weren't perfect in technique, but they were able to get the points and they won the game. Often times in an interview after the game they will say, "It wasn't pretty, but we won."

As Worship Leaders we have to always keep the goal before us and not just the game. I believe in practicing and making your technique as great as you can, but I have to remember that the goal is that the people would connect to God. If this is the goal and we accomplish it, then we shouldn't worry about all the rest of it. So often worship leaders are so worried about making sure the music is perfect, the singers are all on their parts, that no one makes a mistake, and that they get a chance to sing their two new choir songs. In perfecting the "game," they miss the "goal" – creating an opportunity for people to connect to God.

I once overheard a choir director talking with the choir and I quote, "I want you looking at me AT ALL TIMES!" I was disturbed by this because the goal is to get people focused on God and their relationship with Him. If the choir members are only looking at the choir director, when are they looking at JESUS? I have encouraged my chorale to make sure they look at me for where we are going in the song (verse, chorus, etc), but I want them to be leaders in worship as well. I want them to be focused on worshipping God while they sing. People in the church are not just looking at me, but they are looking at the chorale for their response in worship. If the chorale is looking at me, then that is where the church will look also. I want everyone to worship God and to start focusing their minds and actions on Him.

Don't get so concerned with the "game" that you forget the "goal." I spend time working on the game during practice. I will go over and over parts with the chorale and music with the musicians during a practice session. But if we get in service and it doesn't go just perfectly, I don't allow that to get my focus off the goal. When I am in church, the point is that God moves. When He does, I'm done with my part, and it's time for Him to take over.

There have been times when we have learned a new song and been ready to sing it during service that night, but because the flow of the Spirit didn't lead us in that direction, we scrapped it for another night. I want to make sure that worship is the MOST important aspect of our time together and not that we got to sing our new song.

In recent years there has been a growth in the area of worship songs instead of just choir music. I believe this is a good direction, and we strive to do more songs that encourage everyone to worship instead of just enjoy our talents and abilities. In our church, the entire chorale does worship instead of a small group of people. Most of our choir songs (or songs with verses) can be used at any time during the service. We make sure that there is no separation in our church between worship and choir songs. In fact we never announce that it's time for the choir to sing. The choir starts the service in worship and if we do a choir song (something with verses) then you will never know when that transition takes place. We strive to maintain a continual flow and keep the focus on the goal, connecting in worship to Jesus Christ.

Balance is the key word. Strive for excellence in your practice time and that will translate into your performance time. I was reading about Tiger Woods the other day and was amazed to learn something about him. If he is in a tournament, whether he wins or not, he will go from 36 holes of golf to the practice field immediately afterwards. He immediately begins to work on what he felt was his weakness during the game. If he felt his driving was not good, then he goes to the driving range to work on technique and distance. If his putting was off, then he goes to the putting green to work on angles and force. He doesn't worry about it when he is playing in the tournament, but afterwards he goes to a practice session and works on his weaknesses.

It's very important that you get your technique down in practice, but during the game just keep the goal in mind. Don't be discouraged if during service mistakes are made in parts or music. Just worry about that the next time you practice and clean it up then. While you are in church, there is only ONE GOAL – to get people connected in worship with God. Whenever it happens and however it happens, it is the goal, and once you reach that, you have won the game!

Chapter 12

The *Holy of Holies Experience*

      Several months ago, following a three-day fast and a 24-hour prayer chain, I felt the Lord share with me a concept regarding worship. He showed me the Old Testament tabernacle and let me know that what He desires is a "Holy of Holies" experience every time we meet in church. He wants to meet with us and create something deeper than ordinary praise in our services.

      When you study the tabernacle you realize that there were three parts: the outer courts, the Holy Place, and the Holy of Holies. Any Israelite could approach to the outer courts. They could bring their sacrifices and walk into this area. There are many churches that simply meet and sing a few songs, but never really consistently create an atmosphere of deep, connected worship to God. They feel that church is a program or a structured time to meet. Some come just hoping that God takes attendance only and then they can leave to feel as though they have done their part.

The Holy Place was a little different. There were only a selected few people who could enter into this atmosphere where the bread and the lamps were. The men who entered there had gone through a special time of repentance (blood upon the altar) and cleansing (washing in the water bowl). Once they had truly made themselves ready they went into the Holy Place and were in a different arena with God. Here they could actually taste the bread, smell the oil and see the light. This is a deeper connection in worship. These people will come to church and maybe have a special touch of the Spirit upon them. They will connect with God in a deeper realm than just those who "attend." Here you can actually taste the bread (the Word), smell and feel the oil (the anointing), and see things according to the light. They actually do enter into a special place with God, but often they stop short of a full experience in worship.

The Holy of Holies was a very special place. It was reserved for one man only, the high priest, Aaron and his descendants. He spent much effort and time in preparing himself to enter this sacred place. After offering up a sacrifice to cover his sins, he washed himself and his clothing thoroughly. He even checked to make sure there were no tears, or blemishes on his garments or skin. Once he had prepared himself he would step behind that veil into the shekinah presence of God. Here the Spirit of God dwelt like a cloud of smoke and a pillar of fire. He could actually see the manifestation of the presence of God, and I'm sure this was an experience he could never fully relate to others.

God wants to create that kind of experience with us every time we meet together. He desires that our services would feel as though you had entered the Holy of Holies each time. It is possible to do that—if we prepare ourselves with the same process that Aaron went through. As a worship leader, a saint or a minister, we need to prepare ourselves to worship. Through prayer before service we should have a time of repentance. We need to allow God to wash our minds, spirits and hearts during this time. We need to clothe ourselves with the garments of praise. We need to then entertain His Spirit until that atmosphere begins to happen.

Every now and then you may have an "outer court" church service, but you should strive to have a Holy of Holies experience each time you come to church. If we could create this atmosphere through our praise and worship, think of what would happen! We strive to do this in our services, and there are many times that people will receive the Holy Ghost during this time. Healings have occurred, and we have seen true repentance take place in lives.

Please don't just have ordinary service! These are the last days and the last days call for a Holy of Holies church service each week.

Chapter 13

Plow *the Field*

So let me wrap up my thoughts in this book by saying that praise and worship is the key to an effective service. It is not the key to salvation; that comes only from hearing and obeying the Word of God. But if the Word is not preached to people who have truly prepared their heart then it will not take root.

In the parable of the Sower found in Matthew 13, we see that there were four types of ground; (1) ground where the seed could not take root because the fowl of the air came and stole it away, (2) stony ground where there was no depth and it could not take root, (3) thorny ground that was so filled with things that it choked out the good seed and finally (4) the good ground that brought forth fruit. He goes on in Matthew 13:18 and explains each type of ground. The first ground is those that are hearers only of the Word and because they don't have any understanding and obedience to the Word, the enemy is able to come in and actually steal the spoken Word from their hearts and minds. The second ground is someone who is a hearer of the Word and receives it at first with great joy and excitement. Their plan is that whatever is preached, they will obey. But because they never allow the root to go any deeper and take hold in their hearts, at the first sign of trouble or tribulation, that Word dies of their lives. The third ground is someone that is a hearer but is so distracted and consumed by the things of this world – riches, fame, jobs, family relationships, friendships, carnality, personal pleasures – that they allow these things to take root and they eventually choke out all the good Word that has been sown into their lives. But God needs to find those with the fourth type of ground, the good ground. These are people that have not just heard the Word, but are striving to understand and obey, to allow it to take root in their lives so that it will help them to overcome during times of tribulation and persecution. These are those that realize the most important thing they can do is keep less of this world in their lives and more of His Spirit.

I tell you all of that to help you understand that each Sunday our churches are filled with all types of ground. If we allow our Pastor to try and preach the Word or give the "bread of life" to someone who has not prepared the soil, then we are making his job harder. We are causing our Pastor to expend himself to the point of exhaustion and frustration. If we really want to see people's lives changed then we have to give them as much anointed rain of the Spirit into their lives as we possibly can. We have to help them push out carnality and break up the hardness of their hearts to receive the Word. The job of a Worship Leader or Worship Pastor is to help prepare the soil so that when the Word (seed) is sown into their lives it can have every advantage and take root.

Remember that you are not just there to "fill time" until the preaching. And you are not just there to be so technically correct and showcase your own talent. And you are not there to open the doors of your own ministry. Rather you are there as the laborer in the field, preparing the ground, plowing and turning over that hard earth.

I don't know a lot about plowing, but I do realize that it took the farmer to get the job done. There was never a farmer who could hook up the oxen to the plow, set them loose in the field and expect them to get the job done and get it done right! Even today, a farmer, with all the technology at his fingertips, still has to get in the cab of that tractor and keep it moving in the right direction.

Worship leader that is your job! You are responsible for hooking up the oxen to the plow, starting them off in the right place and then holding them in line and getting the job done. Do your best each and every service to make sure that the ground is ready before your Pastor begins to sow the seed.

Yes, I know that it will cost you something. You will have to have a personal walk with Christ on your own. During service, you will be ministering to others and so you will need to make sure that you have filled up your spiritual tank BEFORE you get there. If you feel burned out then the first thing you need to do is go on a fast and prayer cycle for yourself. Get inspired again through the Word. Get some gas in the tank so that you will have something to give to others. There is a lot of prep work that goes into the music and worship department of a church. There are songs to organize, parts to learn and music sessions to work on technique.

But in all that preparation time, don't forget why you are doing all this – you are cleaning the plow and feeding the oxen so that when you get onto the field you are ready to do what God has called you to do.

I pray that whatever aspect of worship you are involved in (leading a service, singing, playing an instrument or just worshipping from the pew), that you will take the lessons and techniques that I have shared in this book. And that you will remember your purpose and you will take on the responsibility of not just telling others what to do, but actually leading them into a personal, intimate, one-on-one talk with Jesus Christ. If you can do that, then your worship services will be revolutionized and your church will be a place where they can come and connect to His presence.

Appendix A

Biblical References to Praise

Deuteronomy 10:21
Deuteronomy 26:19
Judges 5:2-3
1 Chronicles 16:4
1 Chronicles 16:35
1 Chronicles 23:5
1 Chronicles 23:30
1 Chronicles 29:13
2 Chronicles 7:6
2 Chronicles 20:19-22
2 Chronicles 29:30
2 Chronicles 31:2
Ezra 3:10
Nehemiah 9:5
Psalms 7:17
Psalms 9:1-2
Psalms 9:14
Psalms 21:13
Psalms 22:22-26
Psalms 28:7
Psalms 30:12
Psalms 33:1-2
Psalms 34:1
Psalms 35:18
Psalms 35:28

Psalms 40:3
Psalms 42:4-5
Psalms 42:11
Psalms 43:4-5
Psalms 44:8
Psalms 45:17
Psalms 48:10
Psalms 49:18
Psalms 50:23
Psalms 51:15
Psalms 52:9
Psalms 54:6
Psalms 56:4
Psalms 56:10
Psalms 57:7
Psalms 57:9
Psalms 61:8
Psalms 63:3
Psalms 63:5
Psalms 65:1
Psalms 66:2
Psalms 66:8
Psalms 67:3
Psalms 67:5
Psalms 69:30
Psalms 69:34
Psalms 71:6
Psalms 71:8
Psalms 71:14
Psalms 71:22
Psalms 74:21
Psalms 79:13
Psalms 86:12

Psalms 89:5
Psalms 98:4
Psalms 99:3
Psalms 100:1
Psalms 100:4
Psalms 102:18
Psalms 102:21
Psalms 104:33
Psalms 106:1-2
Psalms 106:12
Psalms 106:47-48
Psalms 107:8
Psalms 107:32
Psalms 108:1
Psalms 108:3
Psalms 109:1
Psalms 109:30
Psalms 111:1
Psalms 111:10
Psalms 112:1
Psalms 113:1
Psalms 115:18
Psalms 117:1-2
Psalms 118:19
Psalms 118:21
Psalms 118:28
Psalms 119:7
Psalms 119:164
Psalms 119:171
Psalms 119:175
Psalms 135:1
Psalms 135:3
Psalms 135:21

Psalms 138:1-2
Psalms 138:4
Psalms 139:14
Psalms 142:7
Psalms 145:1-2
Psalms 145:4
Psalms 145:10
Psalms 145:21
Psalms 146:1-2
Psalms 146:10
Psalms 147:1
Psalms 147:7
Psalms 147:12
Psalms 148:1-5
Psalms 148:7
Psalms 148:13-14
Psalms 149:1
Psalms 149:3
Psalms 149:9
Psalms 150
Proverbs 27:21
Isaiah 12:1
Isaiah 12:4
Isaiah 25:1
Isaiah 42:8
Isaiah 42:10
Isaiah 42:12
Isaiah 43:21
Isaiah 48:9
Isaiah 60:18
Isaiah 61:3
Isaiah 61:11
Jeremiah 17:14

Jeremiah 20:13
Jeremiah 33:9
Jeremiah 33:11
Joel 2:26
Zephaniah 3:20
Matthew 21:16
Luke 19:37
Romans 13:3
Philippians 4:8
Hebrews 2:12
Hebrews 13:15
1 Peter 1:7

Appendix B

Biblical Reference to Worship

Genesis 22:5
Exodus 34:14
Deuteronomy 26:10
1 Samuel 15:25
1 Samuel 15:30
2 Kings 17:36
1 Chronicles 16:29
Psalms 5:7
Psalms 22:27
Psalms 29:2
Psalms 45:11
Psalms 66:4
Psalms 86:9
Psalms 95:6
Psalms 96:9
Psalms 99:5
Psalms 99:9
Psalms 132:7
Psalms 138:2
John 4:23-24
John 4:24
Revelation 14:7

Appendix C

Basic Biblical Facts About Praise

When should I praise the Lord?
>Psalm 59:16, *"In the morning I will sing of Your love"*

How often should I praise the Lord?
>Psalm 71:24, *"My tongue will tell of your righteous acts all day long."*

How long should I praise the Lord?
>Psalm 146:2, *"I will praise the Lord at all time; His praise shall continually be on my lips."*

Is church the only place where we praise God?
>Psalm 34:1, *"I will praise the Lord at all times; His praise shall continually be on my lips."*
>Psalm 149:5, *"Let the saints rejoice in this honor and sing for joy on their beds."*

Who are we trying to show His praise to?
>I Chronicles 16:24, *""Declare His glory among the nations, His marvelous deeds among all peoples."*

Psalm 22:22, *"I will declare your name to my brothers; in the congregation I will praise you."*

Can we praise God on the instruments and with music?
Psalm 150:3-5, *"Praise him with the sound of the trumpet: praise him with the psaltery and harp. Praise him with the timbrel and dance: praise him with the stringed instruments and organs. Praise him upon the loud cymbals: praise him upon the high sounding cymbals."*

Is it okay to be loud with our praise?
Psalm 33:3, *"Sing unto him a new song; play skillfully with a loud noise."*
Psalm 98:4, *"Make a joyful noise unto the Lord, all the earth: make a loud noise, and rejoice, and sing praise."*

Made in the USA
Columbia, SC
15 April 2018